Chicago 1933 World's Fair:
A Century of Progress in Photographs

Written by Mark Bussler

Copyright © 2019 Inecom, LLC.
Revised Edition Copyright © 2021 Inecom, LLC.
All Rights Reserved

More books at
CGRpublishing.com

The Clock Book:
A Detailed Illustrated Collection
of Classic Clocks

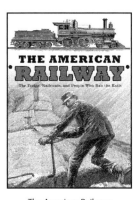

The American Railway:
The Trains, Railroads, and People
Who Ran the Rails

Gustave Doré's London:
A Pilgrimage - Retro Restored
Special Edition

CHICAGO 1933 WORLD'S FAIR: A CENTURY OF PROGRESS IN PHOTOGRAPHS

TABLE OF CONTENTS

010 - Introduction
014 - Chicago 1933
029 - The Fairgrounds
040 - Hall Of Science
059 - Administration Building
064 - Avenue of Flags
071 - U.S. Government Building and Hall of States
094 - The Sky Ride
108 - The Adler Planetarium
114 - Travel and Transport Building
124 - Electrical Building
142 - Company Buildings
166 - The Sinclair Dinosaurs
172 - Other Sights and Sounds

INTRODUCTION

The year was 1833 when a group of hardy individuals founded the city of Chicago on the shore of Lake Michigan. A century later the city wanted to celebrate its growth and the progress of humanity with a fair called "A Century of Progress."

At the time, Americans were proud to be Americans, and the people of Chicago showed great pride in all that Americans had accomplished in the past 100 years. People lauded electricity, steam power, light bulbs, radio, modern medicine, and a national railway system as achievements beyond the imagination of the primitives who existed in an earlier age

It was said that "if Washington could return to our land of railroads and steamboats and airplanes and electricity and telephones and radios and the myriad products of physics and chemistry and biology and geology, he would think that by some magic he had been transported to some marvelous fairyland."

Chicago was no stranger to World's Fairs. Forty years earlier, the city played host to what most people remember as the most revolutionary fair of all, the 1893 Columbian Exposition. More than 22 million people visited the city that summer and spread the wealth to Chicago's merchants, hotels, and transit system. In 1933, in the middle of the Great Depression, there is no doubt that Chicago wanted to try it again.

One individual said that "As is customary in anniversary celebrations, a carnival spirit will prevail, but in addition to fun there will be serious contemplations of the past and sober consideration of the future." Myron E. Adams proposed the fair in 1923, but it took a decade to organize. By 1933, amid an international financial crisis, Chicago was ready to go.

Incredibly, this new Chicago World's Fair would not be taxpayer supported; it was pre-Internet crowdfunded. In April 1928 an invitation was extended to the public to join a legion of World's Fair supporters. Each legionnaire gave $5 and received a certificate exchangeable for ten admissions to the fair. Records show that funding brought in $593,358.

Additionally, offers were made to the public to become members of the corporation. Founder members gave $1000, sustaining members $50. Corporations like General Motors, Chrysler, and Westinghouse Electric were allowed to acquire space at the fair which supplied many additional millions of dollars.

By all accounts, the Century Of Progress Exposition was a resounding success. It was originally planned to run from June to September 1933 but ran a year longer because of its popularity. More than 48 million people visited the fair between May 27, 1933, and October 31, 1934, and, unlike most World's Fairs, it paid for itself.

Aerial view of A Century of Progress!

The directors who created the World's Fair of 1893 envisioned it as a way to reflect America's emergence on the global scene and the architecture reflected that. Artists and craftsmen designed the "White City" of the 1893 Fair to show that the United States was on par with its European rivals and that Chicago was as big Rome and as grand as Paris. The white buildings gleamed with ornate, classic architecture celebrating the greatest cities across Europe.

The 1933 Fair had none of that. In stark contrast to the White City, A Century of Progress was colorful, vibrant, and created in a futuristic art deco fashion to show where America was going rather than where it had been. One writer said, "Planes and curved surfaces characterize these structures instead of a parade of plaster, ornamentation, and decoration."

The fair buildings were built to be temporary and then covered with coats of red, gold, silver and yellow paint. Bright lights accented the structures and spotlights lit up the sky. Electric fountains roared and entertained visitors from all over the world.

Architects designed the exhibit buildings with an absence of windows to emphasize unbroken planes and surfaces. The lack of windows not only saved money, but it gave artists more room to work with artificial light to craft the art deco character of the illumination. When the Fair was over the buildings were razed.

The theme of the Chicago '33 was technology, advancement, and scientific achievement but there was still much room for fun. Instead of a Ferris Wheel, the 1933 fair had the Sky Ride, a massive 600 foot-tall gondola ride over the lagoon and buildings. Visitors to A Century of Progress witnessed a miniature Hollywood, life-size dinosaurs, midway attractions, restaurants, music, exhibitions, talks, and the Pabst Blue Ribbon Casino.

Those fortunate enough to attend A Century of Progress could forget about the troubles of The Great Depression and enjoy all that Chicago and America had to offer.

The 1893 World's Fair in Chicago

CHICAGO 1933

An imposing photograph of Chicago in 1933.

Chicago in 1820.

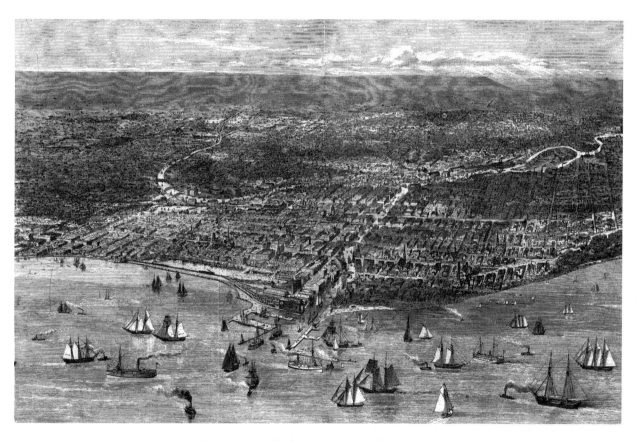

Chicago just before the great fire of 1871.

CIVIC OPERA HOUSE
CHICAGO

TRAFFIC MAP AND GUIDE TO FAIR UTILITIES

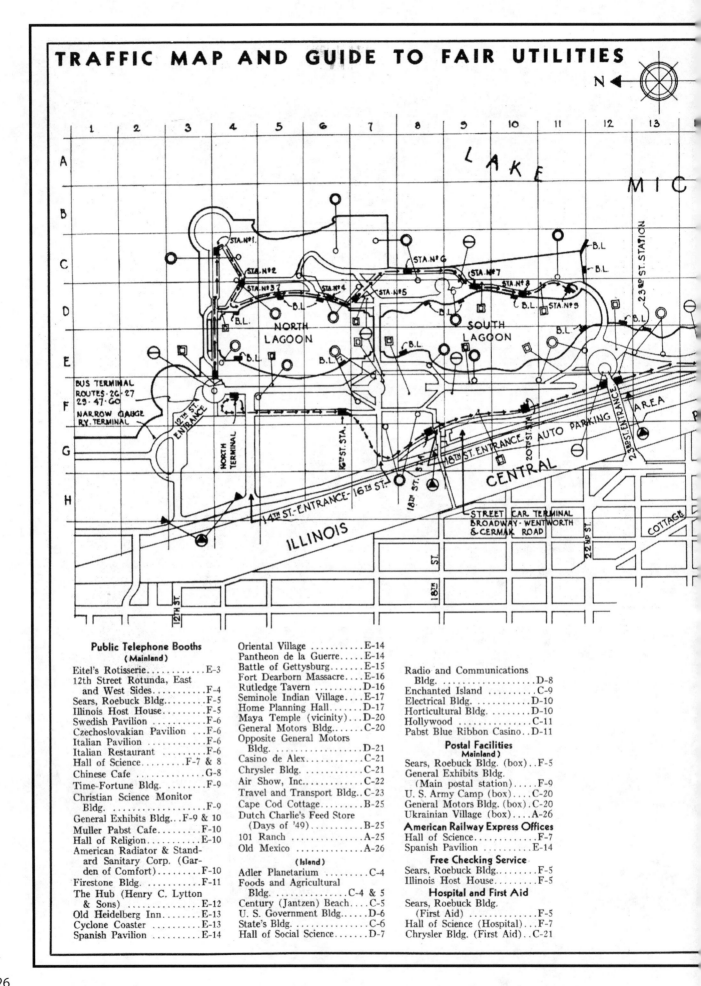

Public Telephone Booths
(Mainland)

Eitel's Rotisserie............E-3
12th Street Rotunda, East and West Sides..........F-4
Sears, Roebuck Bldg.........F-5
Illinois Host House.........F-5
Swedish Pavilion F-6
Czechoslovakian Pavilion ..F-6
Italian Pavilion F-6
Italian Restaurant F-6
Hall of Science........F-7 & 8
Chinese Cafe G-8
Time-Fortune Bldg. F-9
Christian Science Monitor Bldg. F-9
General Exhibits Bldg...F-9 & 10
Muller Pabst Cafe.........F-10
Hall of Religion..........E-10
American Radiator & Standard Sanitary Corp. (Garden of Comfort).........F-10
Firestone Bldg. F-11
The Hub (Henry C. Lytton & Sons) E-12
Old Heidelberg Inn........E-13
Cyclone Coaster E-13
Spanish Pavilion E-14

Oriental Village E-14
Pantheon de la Guerre.....E-14
Battle of Gettysburg......E-15
Fort Dearborn Massacre...E-16
Rutledge Tavern D-16
Seminole Indian Village....E-17
Home Planning Hall.......D-17
Maya Temple (vicinity)...D-20
General Motors Bldg......C-20
Opposite General Motors Bldg. D-21
Casino de Alex...........C-21
Chrysler Bldg............C-21
Air Show, Inc............C-22
Travel and Transport Bldg..C-23
Cape Cod Cottage.........B-25
Dutch Charlie's Feed Store (Days of '49)..........B-25
101 Ranch A-25
Old Mexico A-26

(Island)

Adler Planetarium C-4
Foods and Agricultural Bldg. ....C-4 & 5
Century (Jantzen) Beach...C-5
U. S. Government Bldg....D-6
State's Bldg..............C-6
Hall of Social Science.....D-7

Radio and Communications Bldg. D-8
Enchanted Island C-9
Electrical Bldg. D-10
Horticultural Bldg. D-10
Hollywood C-11
Pabst Blue Ribbon Casino..D-11

Postal Facilities
(Mainland)

Sears, Roebuck Bldg. (box)..F-5
General Exhibits Bldg. (Main postal station).....F-9
U. S. Army Camp (box)....C-20
General Motors Bldg. (box).C-20
Ukrainian Village (box)....A-26

American Railway Express Offices

Hall of Science............F-7
Spanish Pavilion E-14

Free Checking Service

Sears, Roebuck Bldg........F-5
Illinois Host House........F-5

Hospital and First Aid

Sears, Roebuck Bldg. (First Aid)...............F-5
Hall of Science (Hospital)...F-7
Chrysler Bldg. (First Aid)..C-21

26

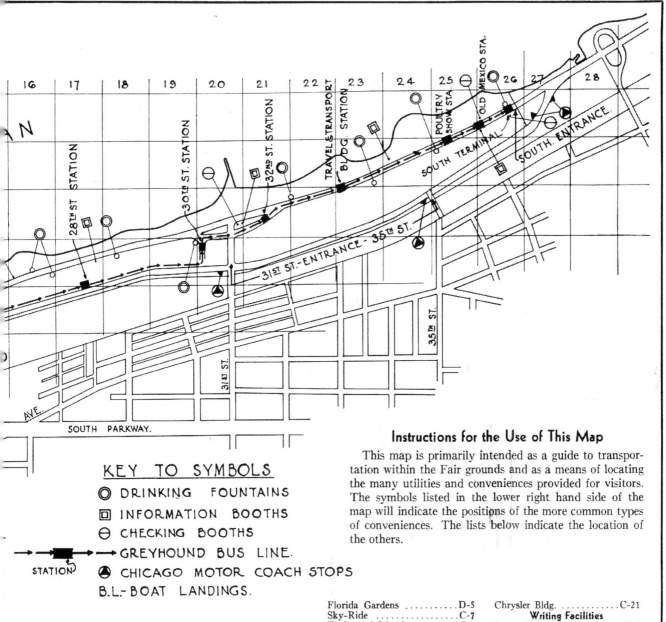

Instructions for the Use of This Map

This map is primarily intended as a guide to transportation within the Fair grounds and as a means of locating the many utilities and conveniences provided for visitors. The symbols listed in the lower right hand side of the map will indicate the positions of the more common types of conveniences. The lists below indicate the location of the others.

KEY TO SYMBOLS
- ⊙ DRINKING FOUNTAINS
- ▣ INFORMATION BOOTHS
- ⊖ CHECKING BOOTHS
- →▬→ GREYHOUND BUS LINE. STATION
- ▲ CHICAGO MOTOR COACH STOPS
- B.L.- BOAT LANDINGS.

Resting Places
(Mainland)
- 12th Street Rotunda........F-4
- Avenue of Flags......F-5, 6 & 7
- Hall of Science..........F-7 & 8
- Japanese Pavilion..........G-7
- Time-Fortune Bldg..........F-9
- Cactus Pergola............F-9
- General Exhibits......F-9 & 10
- American Radiator & Standard Sanitary Corp. (Garden of Comfort).........F-10
- Firestone Building.........F-11
- A & P Carnival............E-13
- Pantheon de la Guerre.....E-14
- North of Bozo.............E-15
- Kohler Pavilion...........E-17
- Home and Industrial Arts Group..................D-17
- Gas Industry Hall.........D-17
- U. S. Army Camp..........D-19
- Maya Temple..............D-20
- General Motors...........C-20
- Chrysler Building........C-21
- Goodyear Field...........B-24

(Island)
- Adler Planetarium.........C-4
- Florida Gardens...........D-5
- Sky-Ride..................C-7
- Enchanted Island..........C-9
- Horticultural Building...D-10
- Hollywood...............C-11

Telegraph Offices
- Sears, Roebuck Bldg........F-5
- Chrysler Bldg............C-21

Traveler's Aid Society
- At 23rd Street Entrance....E-12

Reading and Rest Rooms
- Sears, Roebuck Bldg........F-5
- Illinois Host House........F-5
- Time-Fortune Bldg..........F-9
- Christian Science Monitor Bldg...................F-9
- General Exhibits Bldg...F-9 & 10
- U. S. Steel Reception Room, Pavilon No. 1....F-9
- International Business Machine Corp., Pavilion 3..F-9
- Underwood Typewriter Co., Pavilion No. 3.....F-9
- Elgin Watch Co., Pavilion No. 4..................F-10
- Shelton Looms, Pavilion 5.F-10
- General Cigar Co..........E-12
- General Motors Bldg.......C-20
- Chrysler Bldg.............C-21

Writing Facilities
- Sears, Roebuck Bldg........F-5
- Illinois Host House........F-5
- General Exhibits (U. S. Steel and International Business Machine lounges).........F-9
- Havoline Thermometer....E-12
- Home Planning Hall (Gibson Refrigerating Co. lounge).D-17
- General Motors Bldg.......C-20
- Chrysler Bldg.............C-21

Registration Service
- Sears, Roebuck Bldg........F-5
- Illinois Host House........F-5
- Southern Cypress House....D-17
- Ukrainian Village.........A-26

Lost and Found Department
- General Exhibits Bldg. Connected by 'phone with all information booths on the grounds............F-9

Official Tour Service Booths
- 12th St. Rotunda (N. E. Side).F-4
- Wings of a Century (S. end of building)...........C-23
- Enchanted Island Official children's tours.........C-9

THE FAIRGROUNDS

Chicago's 1933 Fair was big and covered more than 424 acres of prime lakefront real estate within easy walking distance of downtown Chicago. Fairgoers could enjoy the Field Museum, Adler Planetarium, Soldier Field, the Shedd Aquarium, and the lakefront beaches on their visit.

The fairgrounds contained plenty of avenues for walking. Additional modes of transportation included the famous "modern bus service" pictured below.

The colorful buildings, fountains, and lagoons looked nice during the day but by all accounts, A Century of Progress shined most brightly at night. The artistic displays of electric lights gave the fairgrounds a futuristic look that resembled a Buck Rogers comic strip. Beautiful art deco lamps (such as the one pictured on the previous page) dotted the landscape like stars when viewed from above on the Sky Ride.

Fairgoers could spend each day enjoying high brow or low brow entertainment (or some combination of the two) without deviating from the main bus line. Each week featured hundreds of events and a rotating cast of performers and actors.

"How To Enjoy This Week At The Fair" magazine for the week ending on July 23, 1933, recommended that visitors see the "Homes of Tomorrow" exhibit in Home-Planning Hall, the "Way Down South in Mexico" performance and "Beach Delights" with girls in bathing suits.

Hopefully, nobody missed the fashion show at the Blue Ribbon Casino or "Etchings, Engravings, and Lithographs" by Charles Fabens Kelly. Evenings ended with Arcturus Ceremony in the Hall of Science Court and the Venetian Carnival at the Floating Theater.

A reminder for those of you looking to go back in time. 1:30 P.M., July 18, 1933. Blue Ribbon Casino. Don't miss the fashion show.

CENTURY OF PROGRESS
MODERN BUS SERVICE

Fairgoers enjoy a pleasant stroll on a warm day.
The Hall of Science is visible in the background.

HALL OF SCIENCE

MAPS SHOWING EXHIBITS IN HALL OF SCIENCE

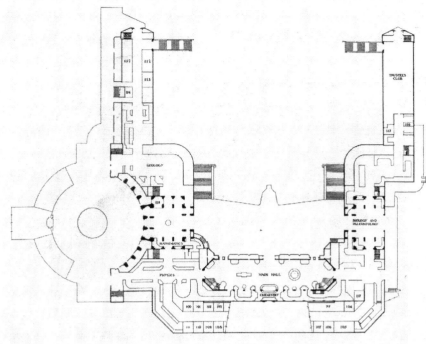

Instructions

The map at the left shows the main, or second floor, and the lower, the ground floor. Official exhibits are marked according to subject matter. Spaces of private exhibitors are numbered and may be located by using the accompanying key.

Main Floor

- 77—State Department of Health
- 100—Chicago Board of Health
- 101—Medical, Dental and Allied Sciences (Women's Division)
- 102—Maternity Center Association
- 103—Occupational Therapy (Good Will Industries)
- 104—Loyola University
- 105—University of Chicago
- 106—American Society for Rheumatism Control
- 107—American Society for Cancer Control
- 108—Chicago Tuberculosis Association
- 109—Chicago Medical Society
- 110—American Heart Association
- 111—Respiration
- 112—Italian Exhibit
- 113—Denmark
- 114—Virginia Geological Service
- 115—Pasteur Institute
- 116—Rommert Microvivarium
- 117—Massachusetts Institute of Technology
- 118—Northwestern Improvement Company

Ground Floor

- 1—Walgreen Drug Store
- 2—Ritter Dental Manufacturing Company
- 3—Chicago Centennial Dental Congress
- 4—Chappel Brothers
- 5—Chicago Pharmaceutical Company
- 6—Reynolds Displaymor Company
- 7—Hospital Library Association
- 8—Mayo Foundation of Rochester, Minn. (Transparent Man)
- 9—American College of Surgeons
- 10—Cleveland Clinic Foundation
- 11—National Oil Products Company
- 12—Thos. J. Dee and Company
- 13—Burton Dixie Company
- 14—Gerber's Baby Products
- 15—Mallinckrodt Chemical Works
- 16—E. R. Squibb and Sons
- 17—Robt. Koch Institute Memorial
- 18—American Medical Association
- 19—Eastman Kodak Company
- 20—Eugene Deitzgen Company
- 21—Taylor Instrument Company
- 22—Hayden Chemical Company
- 23—Dental Supply Co. of New York
- 24—Cruver Manufacturing Company
- 25—Foxboro Company
- 26—Keuffel and Esser
- 27—Federal Products Company
- 28—Simoniz Company
- 29—Russell Playing Card Company
- 30—U. S. Playing Card Company
- 31—Scholl Manufacturing Company
- 32—Massachusetts Institute of Technology
- 33—Bechstein-Moor
- 34—Old Monk Olive Oil
- 35—Victor Chemical Works
- 36—Union Carbide and Carbon Corp.
- 37—August E. Drucker Company
- 38—Bauer and Black
- 39—Merck and Company
- 40—American Optical Company
- 41—Iodent Chemical Company
- 42—Ritter Dental Manufacturing Company
- 43—Pasteur Institute
- 44—Milwaukee Public Museum
- 45—American Pharmaceutical Association
- 46—Bausch and Lomb
- 47—Burroughs and Wellcome
- 48—Heyson, Westcott and Dunning
- 49—W. E. Long Company
- 50—G. D. Searle Company
- 51—Italy
- 52—Municipal Tuberculosis Sanitarium
- 53—American Urological Association
- 54—Wellcome Research Institute
- 55—Hanovia Chemical Company
- 56—Baker and Company, Inc.
- 57—West Disinfecting Company
- 58—Vitamin Food Company
- 59—General Electric X-Ray Corporation
- 60—Abbott Laboratories
- 61—Deiner-Dugas
- 62—Union Carbide and Carbon Company
- 63—Petrolagar (The Doctor)
- 64—Rensaeler Polytechnical Institute
- 65—Hild Floor Machine Company
- 66—Wm. Welch Manufacturing Company
- 67—Union Carbide and Carbon Company
- 68—Dresden Models
- 69—Standard Brands
- 70—Lama Temple Model
- 71—Society for Prevention of Asphyxial Death
- 72—Gaertner Scientific Company
- 73—University of Amsterdam (Holland)
- 74—University of Missouri
- 75—Georgia Warm Springs Foundation
- 76—Model of Byrd's Plane
- 77—University of Illinois
- 78—McGill University
- 79—Marquette University
- 80—Harvard University
- 81—Northwestern University Medical School
- 82—University of Wisconsin
- 83—Allergy Exhibit
- 84—Lyon Metal Products, Inc.
- 85—Bridge World
- 86—Hammond Clock Company
- 87—National Standard Manufacturing Co.
- 88—Green Duck Company
- 89—C. B. Morgan Company
- 90—Western Playing Card Company
- 91—Index Sales Company
- 92—Duplicate Bridge Supply Company
- 93—Bridge Association Office
- 94—U. S. Playing Card Company
- 95—Daily News Public Service
- 96—Kaufmann-Fabry Company
- 97—Stanco—"Flit"
- 98—V. Mueller and Company

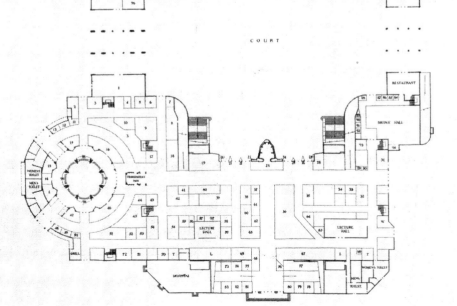

NORTH WING—HALL OF SCIENCE

The theme of Chicago's Century of Progress was science and technology. Consequently one of the fair's most popular and widely photographed buildings was the Hall of Science.

Builders created this massive structure out of numerous sheets of plywood glued together and covered with paint. It was shaped like a "U," which is why this mighty structure looks different from every angle. The Hall of Science included a massive courtyard that hosted talks, displays, and performances.

Organizers filled the building with exhibits that celebrated America's achievements in all things science. Fairgoers witnessed displays filled with scientific achievements in biology, chemistry, geology, mathematics, physics, medical equipment, and progress in drugs and medicine.

In an age when scientific achievements were celebrated instead of feared, this impressive building is one of the most iconic from the 1933 World's Fair.

HALL OF SCIENCE BUILDING
NIGHT VIEW

THE VAST "U-SHAPED" HALL OF SCIENCE

INTERIOR OF GREAT HALL
HALL OF SCIENCE BUILDING

A group of spectators stand in front of the Hall of Science.

NIGHT VIEW OF SOUTH APPROACH HALL OF SCIENCE BUILDING

ADMINISTRATION BUILDING

The organizers of the fair created the Administration Building to be the official headquarters for the exposition which some described as an "experimental laboratory," though not in a nefarious way like it sounds.

This role model for mid-20th-century office buildings showed the future of multi-purpose commercial space with a low cost of construction per foot, high salvage value and easy application for everyday use.

Asbestos cement board formed the exterior walls of Administration Building which provided excellent insulation, particularly considering its lack of windows. Could this building provide the framework upon which architects designed the terrible cheap malls of the 1970s and 1980s?

Sculptures of science and industry dominated the entrance to the building which contained a model of the fair, business space, offices, and the "trustees room."

ADMINISTRATION BLDG.
CHICAGO WORLD'S FAIR – 1933

AVENUE OF FLAGS

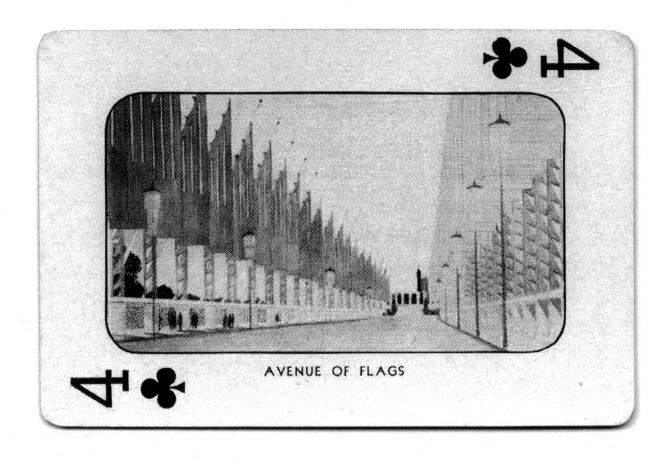

Avenue of Flags.

U.S. GOVERNMENT BUILDING AND HALL OF STATES

The U.S. Government Building was also known as the Federal Building and sat perched upon the spit of land in between the North Lagoon and Lake Michigan.

Like U.S. Government buildings from past fairs, the organizers filled it with displays of America's functioning government, postal service, judiciary system, monetary system, agriculture, and military power.

However, unlike past fairs, the Chicago Century of Progress did away with individual states buildings in favor of the "Hall of States" which sat next to the Federal Building and surrounded a bustling courtyard for talks and performances.

The three fluted towers of the U.S. Government building were creatively lit with indirect and hidden lights to make it one of the most impressive looking and photogenic structures at the fair. The Sky Ride practically ran overhead which provided some amazing aerial views.

Looking North East
Across North Lagoon
Showing U.S.
Government Building
and Agriculture Dome

THE THREE FLUTED TOWERS OF THE FEDERAL BUILDING

Events

1933

2:30 P. M.
Indian Village Ceremonials (continuous through afternoon)

2:45 P. M.
Marjory Hartless Dancing School Tots, Enchanted Island Theatre

3:00 P. M.
"101 Ranch" Wild West Show (also 8:30 p. m.)
Deagan Carillon Selections (also 5, 7, and 9 p. m.)
Chinese Theatre, Joy Fun Toy Company (also 5, 7, 9 and 10:15 p. m.)
Folk dances and songs, Belgian Village Square (also 5, 7, 8:30, 9:30 and 10:30 p. m.)
Girls' and Boys' Play Club of Chicago, Girls' and Boys' Playground, Enchanted Island

3:15 P. M.
Swimming contests and exhibitions, Century (Jantzen) Beach

3:45 P. M.
"The Arts in Chicago, 1893 to 1933," by Dudley Crafts Watson, Art Institute

4:00 P. M.
Films and lecture, Hall of Social Science (also 7:30 p. m.)*
Christian Century Forum, Hall of Religion*

4:15 P. M.
"Legend of the Piper," operetta by Mrs. Archibald Freer (also 5:15)

5:00 P. M.
Orange Blossom Quartet (also 8:30 and 9:30 p. m.). Also Chief Shee-Noo, Indian tenor, 4 and 10 p. m., Florida Exhibit*
U. S. Army Formal Guard Mount: Retreat 5:30 p. m., Camp Whistler*

7:00 P. M.
"Wings of a Century" Pageant
Indian Village Ceremonials (continuous through evening)
Elks Band of Madison, South Dakota, Court of States*
Organ Recital, Meditation Chapel, Hall of Religion*
De La Salle Academy Band Concert, Floating Theatre

7:15 P. M.
3d Field Artillery Band, Camp Whistler*

8:00 P. M.
Mundy Choristers and Olivet Baptist Choir, Floating Theatre*
Heath Film, Illinois Host House

8:35 P. M.
Arcturus Ceremony, Hall of Science Court*

10:00 P. M.
National Council of Women Assembly and Broadcast, Hall of Science Court

*Free admissions

U. S. Government & States Buildings

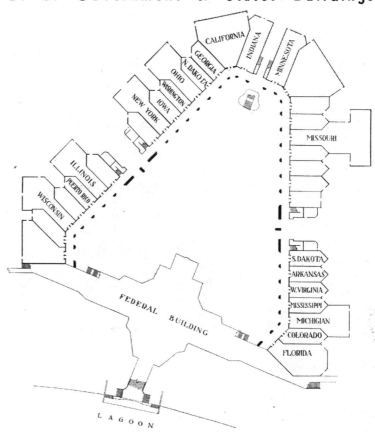

Food and Agricultural Building

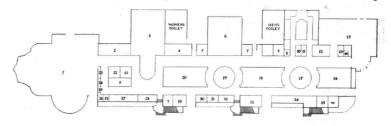

List of Exhibitors in Building

No.	Name	No.	Name
1	International Harvester	19	Standard Brands
2	National Biscuit Co.	20	General Foods
3	Coca-Cola	22	Kerr Glass Mfg. Co.
4	Atlas Brewing	23	Burpee Can Sealer Co.
5	Costa Rica	24	K. Hovden
6	Institute of American Meat Packers	25	W. F. Straub Labs.
7	Stewart & Ashby Coffee	26	Chuckles Candy
8	Ball Bros.	27	National Sugar Ref. Co.
9	Julia King Candy Co.	28	Morton Salt
10	Chr. Hanson Lab. (Junket)	29	P. C. West
11	National Pressure Cooker	30	Kalamazoo Parchment
12	The Glidden Co.	31	Assn. Cooperage Inds. of America
13	Reynolds Appliances	32	Stover Mfg. Co.
14	Urbana Labs.	33	W.L.S. Lounge
15	State of Illinois	34	Libby, McNeill & Libby
16	Quaker Oats Co.	35	Container Corp. of America
17	Kraft Phoenix	T	Telephones
18	H. J. Heinz Co.	W	Century Water Co.

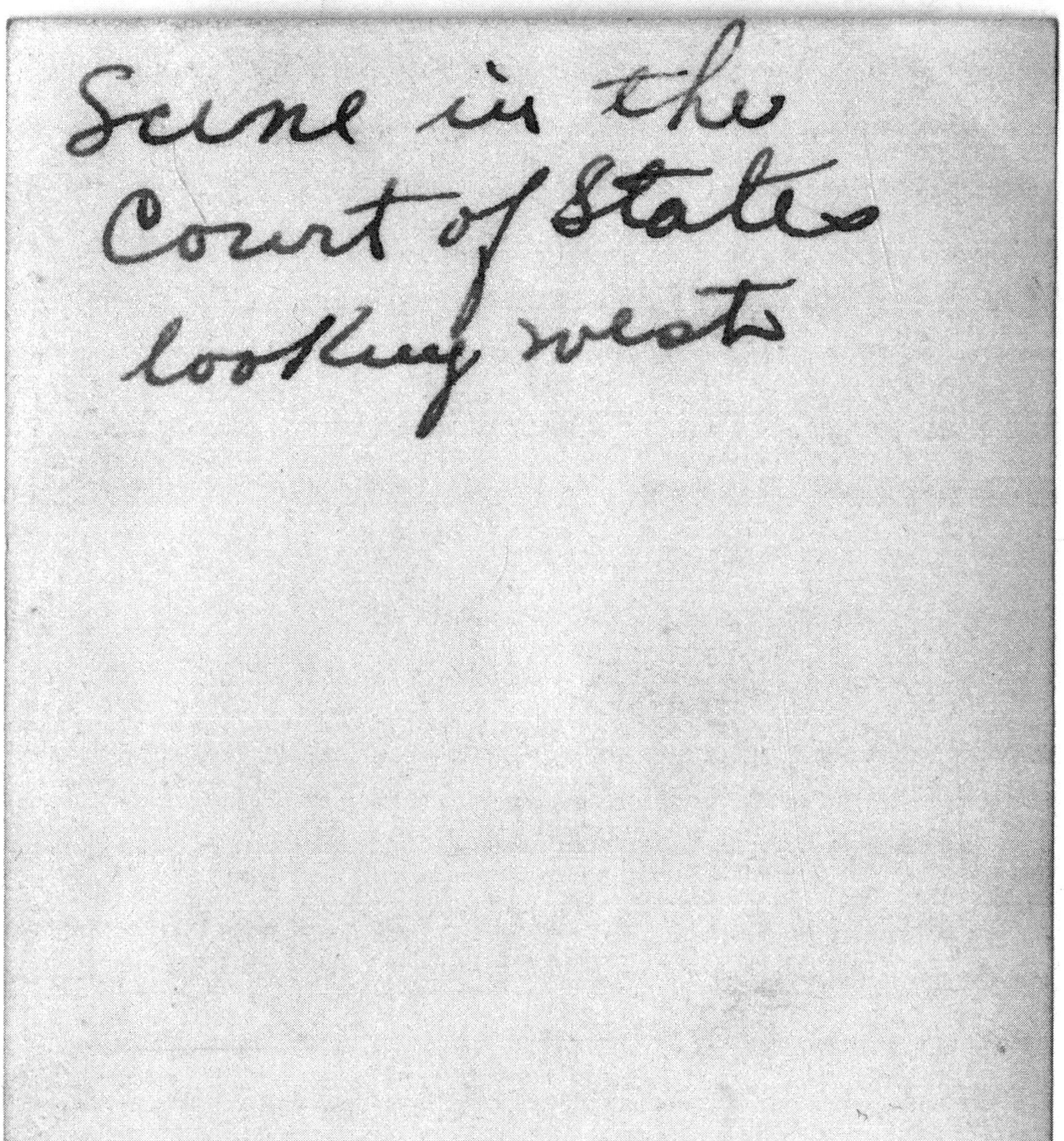

Scene in the
Court of States
looking west

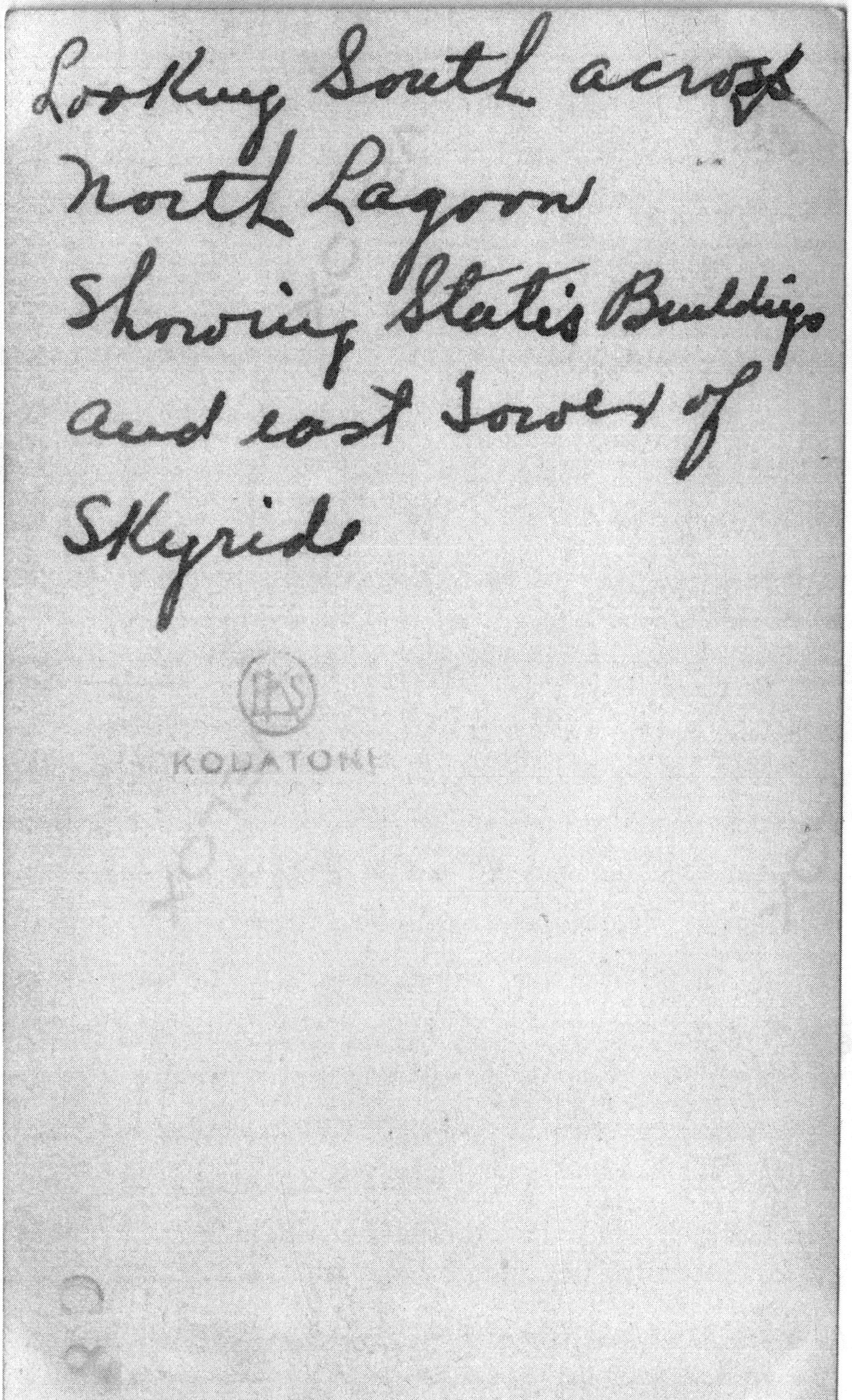

Looking South across
North Lagoon
Showing State's Buildings
and east Tower of
Skyride

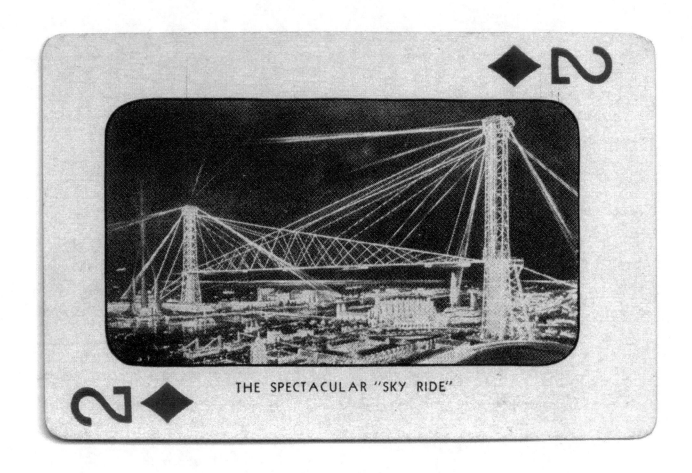

THE SPECTACULAR "SKY RIDE"

THE SKY RIDE

The Sky Ride was 1933's answer to the 1893 Ferris Wheel at the Columbian Exposition. This massive exhibit proved popular at thrilling and terrifying fairgoers brave enough to ride a gondola 200 feet above the lagoon and buildings below.

Its twin towers with observation decks stood more than 600 feet high and connected the mainland with the island housing the U.S. Government Building.

It was said that at the time of its construction the Sky Ride was taller than any other building in Chicago and that only the George Washington bridge exceeded its cableway in length.

1933

A CENTURY OF PROGRESS

SKY-RIDE
SEE THE FAIR FROM THE AIR

SHEDD AQUARIUM
SEARS ROEBUCK BLDG.
SKY RIDE
AVENUE OF FLAGS
JOHN R. THOMPSON'S CASCADES
HALL OF SCIENCE
WONDER BAKE
SWEDEN
LAMA TEMPLE
SWISS VILLAGE
HALL PHOTOG

PARKING SPACE

ERY EXHIBITS · ADLER PLANETARIUM · FOODS AND AGRICULTURE BLDG. · MIDWAY · FEDERAL AND STATES GROUP · HALL OF SOCIAL SCIENCE

DIAN CLUB · ARMOUR & CO. · TIME AND FORTUNE BLDG. · CHRISTIAN SCIENCE MONITOR

RAL EXHIBITS PAVILIONS

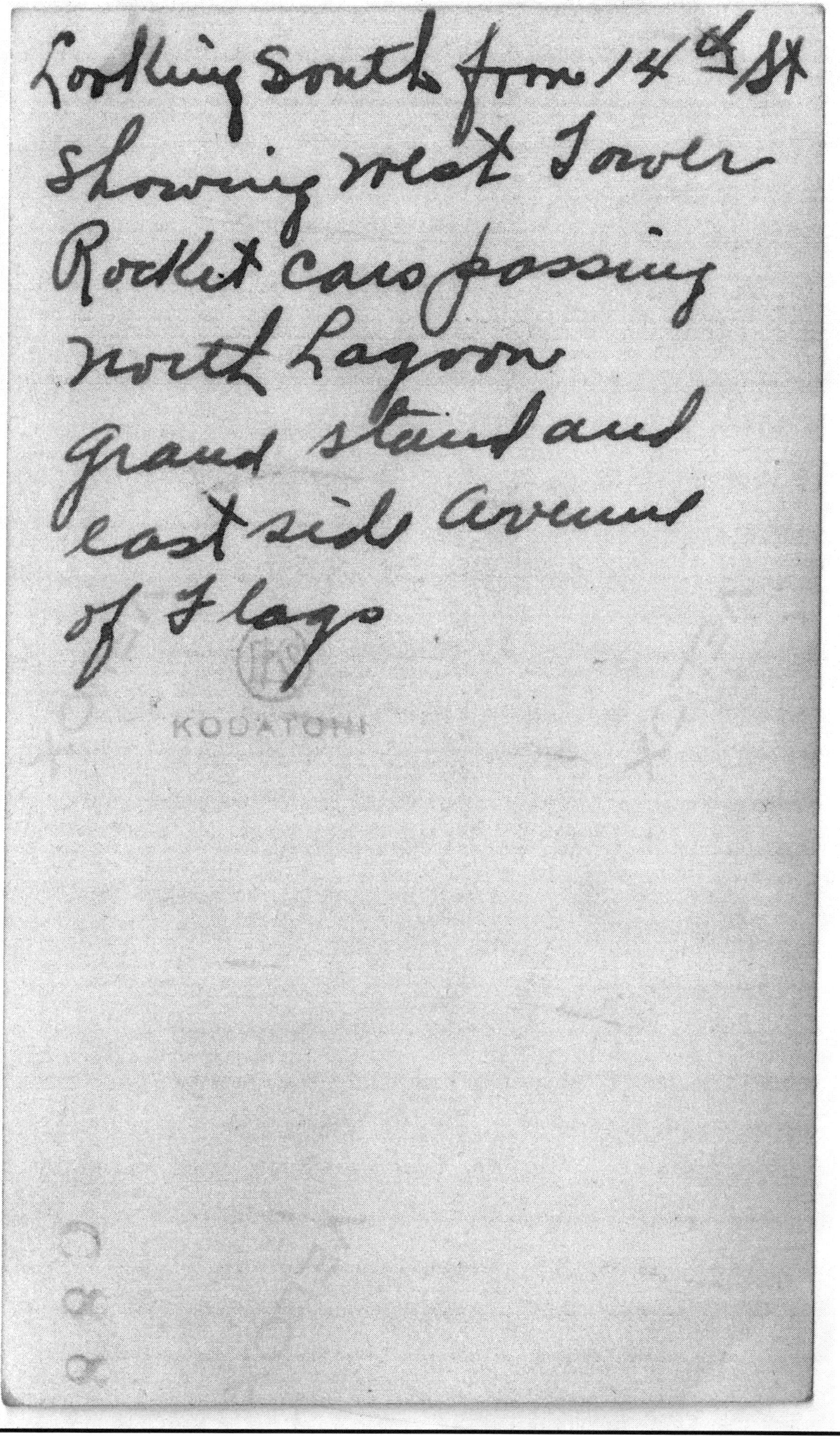
Looking South from 14th St
Showing west Tower
Rocket cars passing
North Lagoon
Grand stand and
east side Avenue
of Flags

KODATONE

THE ADLER PLANETARIUM

Chicago businessman, Max Adler founded the Adler Planetarium in 1930, the first planetarium in the United States. Fairgoers sat beneath its domed roof and watched its artificial sky with projected displays of the sun, moon, and stars.

Like the Field Museum and Shedd Aquarium, the Adler Planetarium was built to be permanent and remains standing to this day in Chicago.

TRAVEL AND TRANSPORT BUILDING

Transportation was a hot subject in 1933, and the Travel and Transport Building was one of the biggest structures at the fair.

This unique building sat on the southern end of the fairgrounds and featured a massive cable suspended dome which was an architectural and engineering achievement at the time. The same principles used to build a suspension bridge hung the roof from twelve towers 125 feet above fairgoers. It created a huge unobstructed space for exhibits.

Modern cars, trains, and planes shared the space with ancient modes of transportation like wagons to celebrate humanity's progress in getting around.

Travel & Transport Bldg.

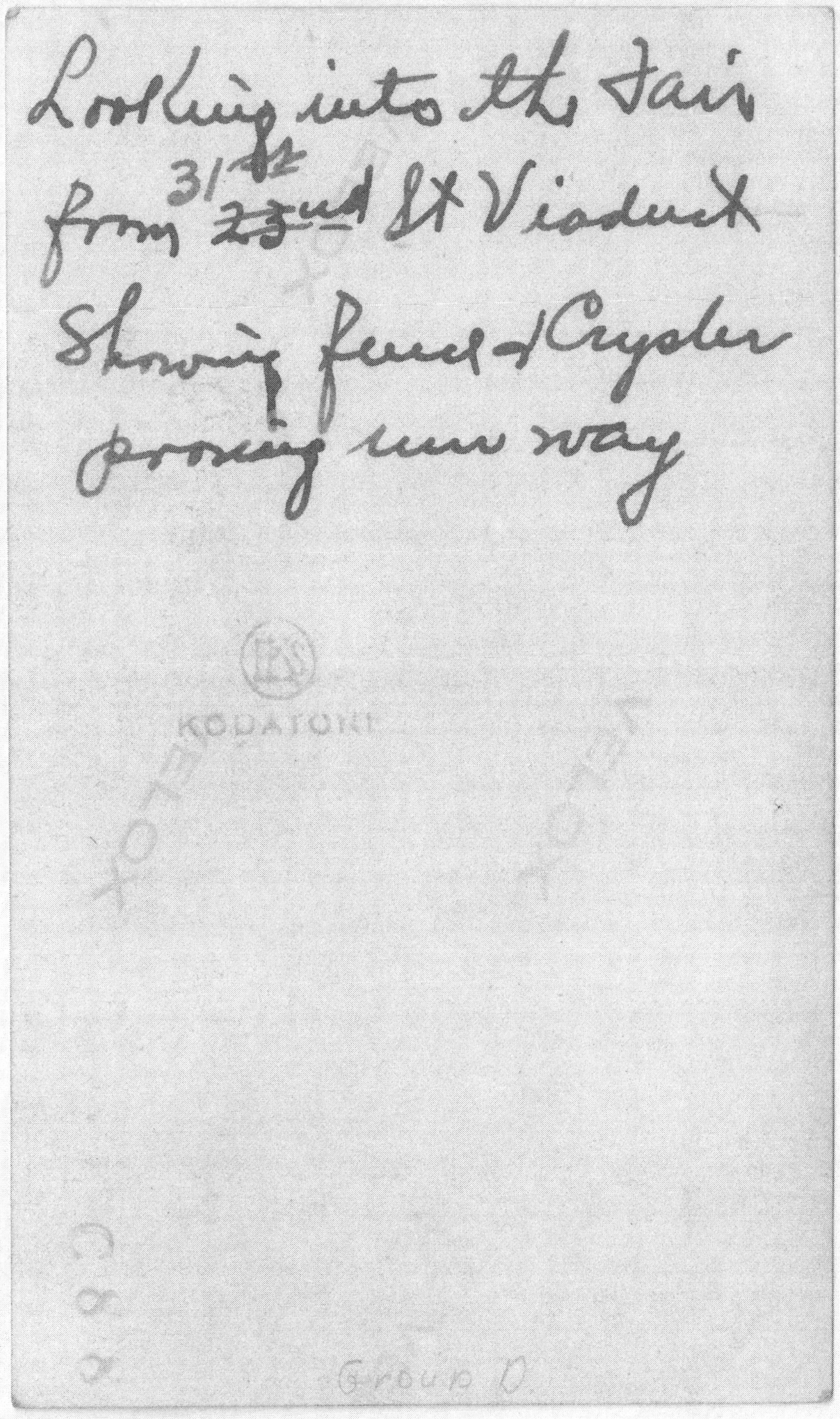

Looking into the Fair
from ~~23rd~~ 31st St Viaduct
Showing fence & Cryoler
proving new way

KODATONE

Group D.

THE ELECTRICAL BUILDING

The 1893 World's Fair in Chicago was the first massive, public display of electric lights in the world. At the end of the 19th century, electricity was new and exciting. Forty years later, in 1933, people no longer viewed electricity as a miracle but rather a tool to be refined and applied to daily use.

Organizers built this brightly lit structure to celebrate the generation, distribution, and utilization of electricity across the country and the world. Massive exhibits, like those of the Westinghouse Electric Company and many others, displayed the rapid advancement of the electric arts in every aspect of life.

Artists covered the silver arc-shaped structure with massive panels that depicted man's struggle to wrest energy from nature. A beautiful electric-powered fountain sat in a courtyard outside the Electrical Building.

Westinghouse Electric Promotional Photographs.

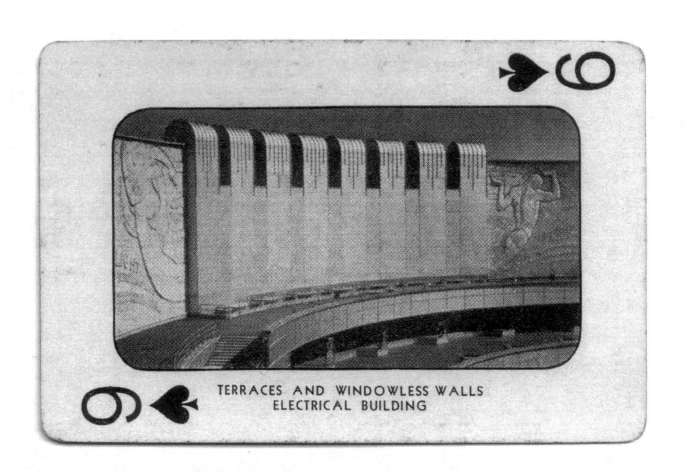

TERRACES AND WINDOWLESS WALLS
ELECTRICAL BUILDING

THE ELECTRICAL GROUP
CHICAGO WORLD'S FAIR
1933

Fountain in Court of Hall of States

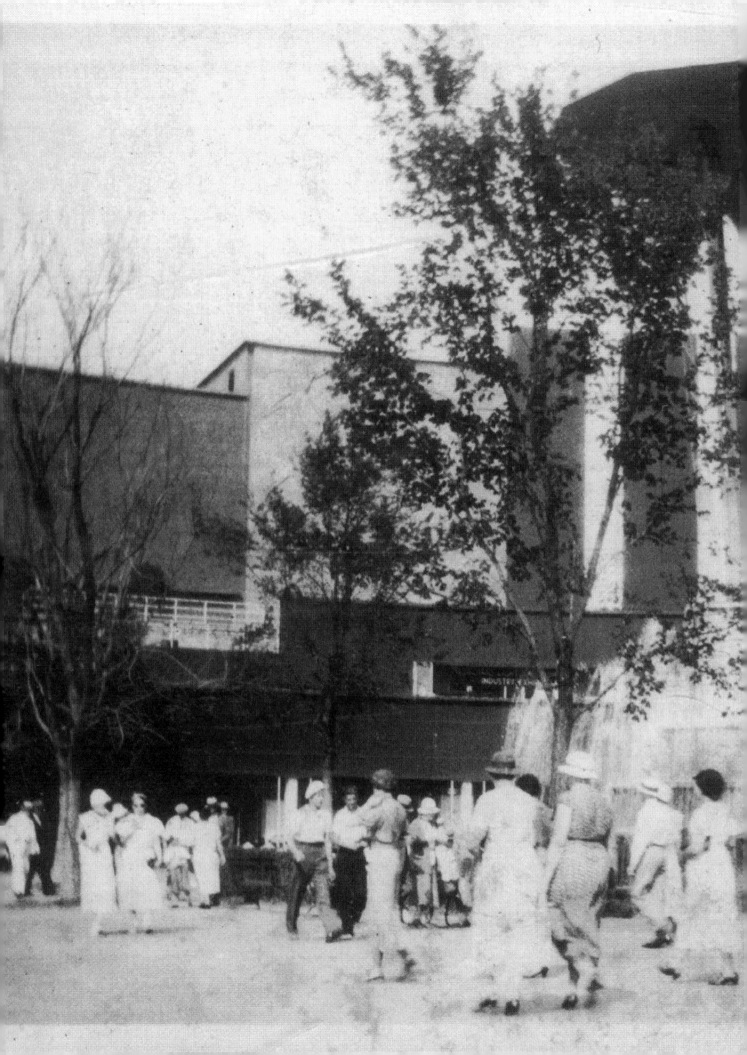

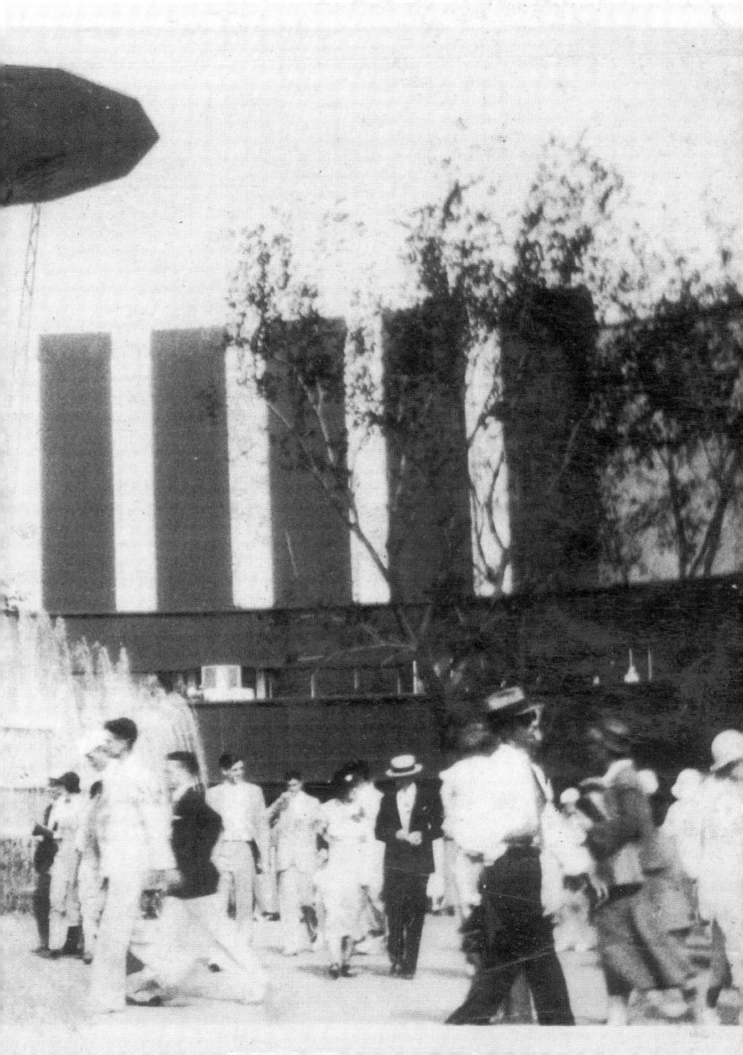

COMPANY BUILDINGS

Many of the largest American companies from the era sponsored the fair like General Motors, Chrysler, Sears Roebuck, Firestone, and Walgreen. They created their own unique and massive structures to promote and advertise their products.

Havoline motor oils constructed a 200-foot tall thermometer which sat in the center of the fairgrounds. Look at the photographs in this book closely because it turns up in the background of many shots.

CHRYSLER BUILDING

GENERAL MOTORS BLDG.
CHICAGO WORLD'S FAIR - 1933

FIRESTONE BUILDING

WALGREEN BUILDING

HORTICULTURAL BUILDING

CHICAGO WORLD'S FAIR EDITION

BIG NEWS

CIRCULATION 1,000,000 — FIRST EDITION

Published by Sinclair Refining Company (Inc.), 45 Nassau Street, New York, N. Y.

SINCLAIR EXHIBITS WEIRD DINOSAURS

Story on Page 2.

PICTURED above is one of the dinosaurs in the Sinclair exhibit at the World's Fair. This is a 25-foot Stegosaurus or Spine-Armored Dinosaur who lived during the Jurassic Period of the Mesozoic Age. This creature had both front and rear brains. The rearmost probably controlled movements of its spine-armor and hind legs. It defended itself with the most weird backbone ever known. At the Sinclair exhibit, Stegosaurus has been re-created in full life size, and is shown in a position as though eating. Note its scaly hide.

SINCLAIR DINOSAUR EXHIBIT AT THE CENTURY OF PROGRESS.
This is Brontosaurus, 40 tons, 70 ft long.

THE SINCLAIR DINOSAURS

The Sinclair Oil exhibit remains one of the most beloved displays from A Century of Progress. Sinclair's logo featured (and continues to feature) a dinosaur that represents their product.

The Sinclair Dinosaurs were life-sized and highly detailed models that towered above visitors. The dinosaur exhibit sat near the Firestone building and was hugely popular with children and adults alike.

OTHER SIGHTS AND SOUNDS

Numerous other buildings such as the General Exhibits Group, the Hall of Social Sciences, the Hall of Religion, the Agriculture Building, and Illinois Building dotted the fairgrounds and played host to displays, performances, and daily spectacles.

Intertwined with the larger structures were smaller, but no less impressive displays such as Admiral Byrd's South Pole Ship, Old Heidelberg, The Enchanted Island, Belgium Village, The Thomas Edison Memorial, the Golden Pavilion of Jehol, the replica of Old Fort Dearborn and much more.

Those fortunate fairgoers who managed to travel to the Chicago World's Fair of 1933 could spend a lifetime exploring, eating, and gawking at the seemingly endless list of things to do and places to eat!

Monday's Events
July 17, 1933

STARTS POLISH HOSPITALITY WEEK
9:30 A. M.
    Art Institute Tour, Helen Barsaloux. "Italian Old Masters," by Helen Parker (11:a.m.)
10:00 A. M.
    All Midway Concessions Open
    "Drama of the Heavens," Demonstrations hourly to 10 p. m., Adler Planetarium
11:00 A. M.
    Lecture and film, Hall of Science (also 2, 4, and 7 p. m.)*
    Demonstration school classes, under auspices of Board of Education and Social Science Division (also 12:00 Noon), Hall of Social Science*
    Lucille Coffey Dancers' Revue, Enchanted Island Theatre
11:20 A. M.
    A & P Carnival: Marionette Show (also 12:20, 1:20, 3, 5:30, 7:30 and 10:30 p. m.). Concerts at 4 and 8:30 p. m., dance music at 5 and 10 p. m.*
11:45 A. M.
    Tony Sarg's Marionettes, Enchanted Island Theatre (also 1:15 and 6:15 p. m.)
12:15 P. M.
    "What to See on a First Visit to the Exhibition," by Helen F. Mackenzie, Art Institute
    Off-The-Street-Club, East of Court of States (also 3 and 5 p. m.)
12:30 P. M.
    Animal Show, Pamahasika's Pets, Enchanted Island Theatre (also 2:45 and 7:00 p.m.)
1:30 P. M.
    Fashion Show, Blue Ribbon Casino*
2:00 P. M.
    Organ Recital, Meditation Chapel, Hall of Religion*
    Bridge Session, Hall of Science (also 8:00 p. m.)*
    "Chronicles of America," historical film, Hall of Social Science*
    "The Art of Titian," by Dudley Crafts Watson, Art Institute
    "The Singing Lady," Boys' Playground, Enchanted Island
    Intercollegiate Chess Tournament, Hall of Science*
    "Knave of Hearts," Esther Sachs, American Conservatory, Enchanted Island Theatre
2:30 P. M.
    Indian Village Ceremonials (continuous through afternoon)
3:00 P. M.
    "101 Ranch" Wild West Show (also 8:30 p. m.)
    Musical Selections, Deagan Carillon (also 5, 7, and 9 p. m.)
    Chinese Theatre, Joy Fun Toy Company (also 5, 7, 9 and 10:15 p. m.)
    Folk dances and songs, Belgian Village Square (also 5, 7, 8:30, 9:30 and 10:30 p. m.)
    U. S. Army Escort to Standard and Band, Camp Whistler*
    Off-The-Street-Club, Foreign Dances, Girls' Playground Enchanted Island
    Health Films Illinois Department of Health, Illinois Host House
3:15 P. M.
    Swimming contests and exhibitions, Century (Jantzen) Beach
3:30 P. M.
    Chicago Story League Group Plays, Enchanted Island Theatre
3:45 P. M.
    "Modern Paintings, How to Enjoy Them," by Dudley Crafts Watson, Art Institute
4:00 P. M.
    Films and lecture, Hall of Social Science (also 7:30 p. m.)*
    U. S. Army Dress Parade, Camp Whistler*
4:15 P. M.
    "Legend of the Piper," by Mrs. Archibald Freer (also 5:15 p. m.)
5:00 P. M.
    Orange Blossom Quartet (also 8:30 and 9:30 p. m.). Also Chief Shee-Noo, Indian Tenor, at 4 and 10 p. m., Florida Exhibit*
    U. S. Army Formal Guard Mount; Retreat 5:30 p. m., Camp Whistler*
7:00 P. M.
    "Wings of a Century" Pageant (three continuous shows)
    Indian Village Ceremonials (continuous through evening)
7:15 P. M.
    3d Field Artillery Band, Camp Whistler*
8:00 P. M.
    Walther League Assembly and Concert, Hall of Science Court*
8:30 P. M.
    Piccard Compton ascension ceremonies, Soldier Field
9 P. M.
    Umbrian Glee Club, Negro Spirituals, Floating Theatre*
10:30 P.M.
    Piccard Balloon ascension (subject to weather conditions)

*Free admissions

GUIDE To Fair Entrances and Transportation

● How do you get to the World's Fair Grounds, and how do you get about once you are there?

The following information will tell you and help you to decide which entrance to the Fair grounds best suits your purpose and convenience:

North or Twelfth Street Entrance
Reached by I. C., bus, miniature railway and auto, but no parking. Main taxi entrance. Nearest Elevated station, Roosevelt Road.
Chief features nearby:
  Administration Building
  Soldier Field
  Sears, Roebuck Building
  Illinois Host House
Approach to Northerly Island, comprising:
  Adler Planetarium
  Dairy Building
  Foods and Agricultural Building
  Century (Jantzen) Beach

Fourteenth Street Entrance
Private car entrance for loading and unloading. No parking.

Eighteenth Street Entrance
Reached by street cars, taxis, I. C., bus, and autos. Cars may be parked nearby for a fee. Nearest Elevated station, five blocks. Nearest entrance to Science bridge, leading to Northerly Island.
Chief features nearby:
  Hall of Science
  Japanese Pavilion
  Chinese Pavilion
  Sky-Ride
  Time-Fortune Building
  General Exhibits Group
  Italian Pavilion
  Submarine S-49
  Swedish Pavilion
  Czechoslovakian Pavilion
  Showboat
  Lama Temple
  Christian Science Monitor Building

Twenty-Third Street Entrance
Reached by street cars, I. C., taxis, bus, and autos. Best automobile approach. Cars may be parked for a fee.
Chief features nearby:
  Firestone Building
  Belgian Village
  Moroccan Village
  Streets of Paris
  A & P Carnival
  Infant Incubator
  Sinclair Prehistoric Exhibit
  Hall of Religion
  Byrd Ship
  World a Million Years Ago

Thirty-First Street Entrance
Reached by street cars, I. C., taxis, bus, and autos. Free parking in streets nearby.
Chief features nearby:
  General Motors Building
  Chrysler Motors Building
  Maya Temple
  Indian Village
  Home and Industrial Arts Group
  U. S. Army Camp
  Wings of a Century
  Travel and Transport Building
  Air Show

Thirty-Fifth Street Entrance
Foot bridge across I. C. tracks, bus stop.
Chief features nearby:
  Whiting Corp.—Nash Motors Building
  Outdoor Railroad Exhibit
  Machinery Demonstration Area
  Poultry Show
  Days of '49
  Domestic Animal Show

South Entrance (37th Street)
Convenient for both north and south traffic. Parking for a fee.
  Reached by auto, bus, and taxi.
Chief features nearby:
  Great Beyond
  Ukrainian Pavilion
  101 Ranch
  Rolleo (Log-Rolling)
  Mexican Village

Within the Grounds

Mainland Bus Service
Via high speed road from North entrance. Dime turnstiles admit passengers to Stations one to ten. Cashiers collect fares beyond 31st street.

Station one—Sixteenth street:
  Sky-Ride
  North End Hall of Science
  Lama Temple
  Japanese Pavilion
  Chinese Pavilion
  Swedish Pavilion
  Italian Pavilion
  Czechoslovakian Pavilion
  Submarine S-49
Station two—Eighteenth street:
  Hall of Science
  General Exhibits Group
  Time-Fortune Building
  Christian Science Monitor Building
Station three:
  General Exhibits Group
  Showboat
  Hall of Religion
  Garden of Comfort
Station four—Twenty-third street:
  Firestone Building
  World a Million Years Ago
  Havoline Thermometer
  Sinclair Prehistoric Exhibit
  Infant Incubator
Station five:
  Belgian Village
  Streets of Paris
  Moroccan Village
  A & P Carnival
Station six:
  Center of Midway Attractions
Station seven:
  South end of Midway
  Home and Industrial Arts, model houses.
Station eight:
  Maya Temple
  Indian Village
  U. S. Army Camp
Station nine—Thirty-first street:
  General Motors Building
  Chrysler Motors Building
  Travel and Transport Building
Station ten:
  Air Show
  Travel and Transport Building
  Wings of a Century
  Whiting Corp.—Nash Motors Building

Tuesday's Events
July 18, 1933

KANSAS DAY

9:30 A. M.
  General Tour of Art Institute, conducted by Helen Barsaloux. "English 18th Century Painting," by Helen Parker (11:00 a. m.)
10:00 A. M.
  "Drama of the Heavens," Demonstrations hourly to 10 p. m., Adler Planetarium
11:00 A. M.
  Films and lecture, Hall of Science (also 2, 4, and 7 p. m.)*
  Dental Puppet Show, Hall of Science (also 2 and 4 p. m.)*
  Demonstration classes, Hall of Social Science, Board of Education.*
11:20 A. M.
  A & P Carnival: Marionette Show (also 12:20, 1:20, 3, 5:30, 7:30 and 10:30 p. m.).
  Concerts at 4 and 8:30 p. m., and dance music at 5 and 10 p. m.*
11:45 A. M.
  Tony Sarg's Marionettes, Enchanted Island Theatre (also 2 and 6:15 p. m.)
12:15 P. M.
  "Common Sense in Paintings," by George Buehr, Art Institute
  Girl Reserves, Outdoor Area, Court of States (also 3 and 5 p. m.)
12:30 P. M.
  Junior League's "Cinderella," Enchanted Island Theatre (also 2:45 p. m.)
1:15 P. M.
  Animal Show, Pamahasika's Pets, Enchanted Island Theatre (also 3:30 and 7 p. m.)
1:30 P. M.
  Fashion Show, Blue Ribbon Casino*
2:00 P. M.
  Bridge Session, Hall of Science (also 8:00 p. m.)*
  "Chronicles of America," historical film, Hall of Social Science*
  "From El Greco to Van Gogh; Paintings of Emotion," by George Buehr, Art Institute
  Intercollegiate Chess Tournament, Hall of Science*
2:30 P. M.
  Indian Village Ceremonials (continuous through afternoon)
  Groves and Company Band, Flint, Michigan, Electrical Building Court*
3:00 P. M.
  "101 Ranch" Wild West Show (also 8:30 p. m.)
  Deagan Carillon Selections (also 5, 7, and 9 p. m.)
  Chinese Theatre, Joy Fun Toy Company (also 5, 7, 9 and 10:15 p. m.)
  Folk dances and songs, Belgian Village Square (also 5, 7, 8:30, 9:30 and 10:30 p.m.)
  U. S. Army Formal Guard Mount, Camp Whistler*
  Creative Dramatics, Miss Ward of Evanston, Girls' Playground, Enchanted Island
  International Council of Religious Education Hour, Hall of Religion*
3:15 P. M.
  Swimming contests and exhibitions, Century (Jantzen) Beach
3:45 P. M.
  "Etchings, Engravings and Lithographs," by Charles Fabens Kelley, Art Institute
4:00 P. M.
  Film and lecture, Hall of Social Science (also 7:30 p. m.)*
  Afternoon Musicale, National Council of Women's Clubs, Hall of Social Science*
  U. S. Army Dress Parade, Camp Whistler*
4:15 P. M.
  "Legend of the Piper," Enchanted Island Theatre (also 5:15 p. m.)
5:00 P. M.
  Orange Blossom Quartet (8:30 and 9:30 p. m.), also Chief Shee-Noo, Indian Tenor, at 4 and 10 p. m., Florida Exhibit*
  U. S. Army Formal Guard Mount: Retreat at 5:30 p. m., Camp Whistler*
7:00 P. M.
  "Wings of a Century" Pageant (three continuous shows)
  Indian Village Ceremonials (continuous through evening)
  Organ Recital, Meditation Chapel, Hall of Religion*
7:15 P. M.
  6th Infantry Band, Camp Whistler*
  Groves and Company Band, Flint, Michigan, Hall of Science Court*
8:00 P. M.
  Operatic Program, Floating Theatre*
8:35 P. M.
  Arcturus Ceremony, Hall of Science Court*
9:00 P. M.
  Hollywood Program, featuring Alice Mock and Edgar Guest.
9:15 P. M.
  Venetian Carnival, Floating Theatre

*Free admissions

THE ILLINOIS BLDG.
CHICAGO WORLD'S FAIR
1933

Belgium Village

ADMIRAL BYRD'S SOUTH POLE SHIP—"CITY OF NEW YORK"

Admiral Byrds South

lar Ship

SOLDIER FIELD STADIUM AND
CHICAGO SKY LINE

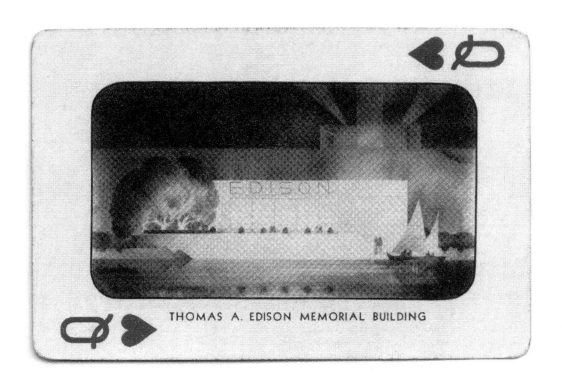

GOLDEN PAVILION OF JEHOL

ELEVATION OF HORTICULTURAL BUILDING

BUILDING OF POLAND

INTERIOR OF JEHOL PAVILION CHICAGO WORLD'S FAIR - 1933

ORIENTAL VILLAGE

AMUSEMENTS

ORIENTAL VILLAGE – CHICAGO WORLD'S FAIR – 1933

OTHER BOOKS FROM CGR PUBLISHING AT CGRPUBLISHING.COM

1939 New York World's Fair: The World of Tomorrow in Photographs

San Francisco 1915 World's Fair: The Panama-Pacific International Expo.

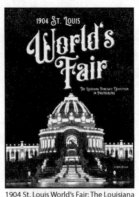
1904 St. Louis World's Fair: The Louisiana Purchase Exposition in Photographs

1915 San Francisco World's Fair in Color: Grandeur of the Panama-Pacific...

19th Century New York: A Dramatic Collection of Images

The American Railway: The Trains, Railroads, and People Who Ran the Rails

The Aeroplane Speaks: Illustrated Historical Guide to Airplanes

The World's Fair of 1893 Ultra Massive Photographic Adventure Vol. 1

The World's Fair of 1893 Ultra Massive Photographic Adventure Vol. 2

The World's Fair of 1893 Ultra Massive Photographic Adventure Vol. 3

Henry Ford: My Life and Work - Enlarged Special Edition

Magnum Skywolf #1

Ethel the Cyborg Ninja Book 1

The Complete Ford Model T Guide: Enlarged Illustrated Special Edition

How To Draw Digital by Mark Bussler

Best of Gustave Doré Volume 1: Illustrations from History's Most Versatile...

OTHER BOOKS FROM CGR PUBLISHING AT CGRPUBLISHING.COM

Ultra Massive Video Game Console Guide Volume 1

Ultra Massive Video Game Console Guide Volume 2

Robot Kitten Factory

The Classic Guide to Still-Life and Figure Drawing

Antique Cars and Motor Vehicles: Illustrated Guide to Operation...

Chicago's White City Cookbook

The Clock Book: A Detailed Illustrated Collection of Classic Clocks

The Complete Book of Birds: Illustrated Enlarged Special Edition

1901 Buffalo World's Fair: The Pan-American Exposition in Photographs

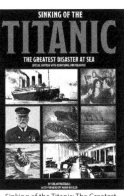
Sinking of the Titanic: The Greatest Disaster at Sea

Gustave Doré's London: A Pilgrimage: Retro Restored Special Edition

Milton's Paradise Lost: Gustave Doré Retro Restored Edition

The Art of World War 1

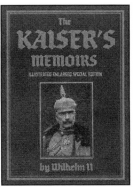
The Kaiser's Memoirs: Illustrated Enlarged Special Edition

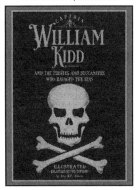
Captain William Kidd and the Pirates and Buccaneers Who Ravaged the Seas

The Complete Butterfly Book: Enlarged Illustrated Special Edition

- MAILING LIST -
JOIN FOR EXCLUSIVE OFFERS

www.CGRpublishing.com/subscribe

Made in the USA
Monee, IL
03 November 2024

dd4c5fca-96de-43a9-be5f-5c0ca65edd68R01